Invincible Ink

Invincible Ink

Poems by
Don Gutteridge

First Edition

Hidden Brook Press
www.HiddenBrookPress.com
writers@HiddenBrookPress.com

Invincible Ink
by Don Gutteridge

Cover Design – Sol Terlson Kennedy
Layout and Design – Richard M. Grove

Typeset in Garamond
Printed and bound in USA
Distributed in USA by Ingram,
        in Canada by Hidden Brook Distribution

Library and Archives Canada Cataloguing in Publication

Title: Invincible ink / Poems by Don Gutteridge.
Names: Gutteridge, Don, 1937- author.
Identifiers: Canadiana (print) 20200406876 |
        Canadiana (ebook) 20200406892 |
                ISBN 9781989786246 (softcover) |
                ISBN 9781989786253 (ebook)
Classification: LCC PS8513.U85 I58 2020 |
        DDC C811/.54—dc23

For Art and Jim:
good friends,
friends of poetry.

Contents:

– Litmus – *p.1*

– Carpe Diem – *p. 2*

– Dithyramb – *p.3*

– Flood – *p.4*

– High – *p.5*

– Thorns – *p.6*

– God's Good Humour – *p.7*

– Stuck – *p.8*

– Tooth and Claw – *p.9*

– Wintering – *p.10*

– Squeeze – *p.11*

– Arrival – *p.12*

– Dixie – *p.13*

– Marooned – *p.14*

– When Love Harrows – *p.15*

– Mooch – *p.16*

– Wings – *p.17*

– Galleon – *p.18*

– Fledgling – *p.19*

– Marybelle – *p. 20*

– The Day I Fell in Love – *p.21*

– Fiefdom – *p.22*

– Local – *p.23*

– Beyond Blood and Bone – *p.24*

– Spare Parts – *p.25*

– Rinsed – *p.26*

– Neighbourhood – *p.27*

– Truce – *p.28*

– A Walk in the Park – *p.29*

– Gusts – *p. 30*

– Groomed – *p.31*

– Aglow: Waterloo County October 1961 – *p.32*

– Soothed – *p.33*

– Strolling Canatara – *p.34*

– At Home – *p.35*

– Bid – *p.36*

– On the Wane – *p.37*

– Bellow – *p.38*

– Ballet – *p.39*

– Our Team – *p. 40*

– Bridal – *p.41*

– Into the April Morning – *p.42*

– Green World – *p.43*

– Date – *p.44*

– Bridal – *p.45*

– A Love Poem – *p.46*

Fifteen for Anne

– Furious Felicity – *p.48*

– Vistas – *p.49*

– Vintage – *p. 50*

– Numinous – *p.51*

– Moonstruck – *p.52*

– Longitudes – *p.53*

– Free – *p.54*

– Harmony – *p.55*

– Buzz – *p.56*

– Id – *p.57*

– Unexempt – *p.58*

– Ardour – *p.59*
– Compromise – *p. 60*
– Joust – *p.61*
– Legacies – *p.62*

Fifty for Tom

– A Summer Day – *p.64*
– Livid – *p.65*
– Faith – *p.66*
– This Day – *p.67*
– Mellow – *p.68*
– Hazard – *p.69*
– Agape – *p. 70*
– Going – *p.71*
– Majestic – *p.72*
– Brevity – *p.73*
– Seasons – *p.74*
– Odes – *p.75*
– Beryl – *p.76*
– Jewelled – *p.77*
– In the Bone – *p.78*
– Throttled – *p.79*
– Prime – *p. 80*
– Stung – *p.81*
– Autumns – *p.82*
– Brave – *p.83*
– Abode – *p.84*
– All Things – *p.85*
– Teem – *p.86*
– Glisten – *p.87*

– Buoyant – *p.88*

– Baptism – *p.89*

– Dream – *p. 90*

– Muppetry – *p.91*

– Hallowed – *p.92*

– One Wish – *p.93*

– Above Cyprus – *p.94*

– Possibility – *p.95*

– Such Days – *p.96*

– Someone Else – *p.97*

– Never Enough – *p.98*

– Meadow – *p.99*

– Cherished – *p. 100*

– Milestone – *p.101*

– Pedigrees – *p.102*

– Insurrection – *p.103*

– Good Night – *p.104*

– When God's Stalked – *p.105*

– Back-Lit – *p.106*

– Hug – *p.107*

– Homage – *p.108*

– Astride – *p.109*

– Cousins – *p.110*

– Fall – *p.111*

– Capture – *p.112*

– O Beautiful Boy – *p.113*

Author Bio Note – *p.115*

Litmus

The urge to pen a poem
is as old as the lullaby sung
to ease the sleep of a fretting
child or the heartfelt hymn
to an ungrateful god or a
soliciting psalm to the setting
sun, for a poem, ancient
or newly honed, is really
a surging of the soul towards
the litmus of light or the mind
on the brink of begetting: words
stirred afoot, seasoned
with invincible ink.

Carpe Diem

With a nod to Ogden Nash

Horace urged us all
To "Seize the day!" or
for those with a yen for the Latin
lingo. "Carpe diem,"
and Herrick preferred gathering
rosebuds while we may.
but I have always plucked
the fulsome flower and that
is the difference between him and me-um.

Dithyramb

A dream: Tom and I
cruising our blue-bellied
Lake in my uncle's 'punt,'
enthused by a ten-horse
Evinrude and pursued by herring
gulls greedy for anything
gilled, and in a far bay
we weigh anchor and drop
our worm-wriggled lines
into the chilled chambers below,
where jut-jawed bass
as muscled as muskies lurk
assertive, and the day just
drifts by as soothing as an
afternoon snooze,
and we hearken to the dithyrambic
rhythms of the heart, and I pray
this dream will never darken.

Flood

When God's sudden flood
sent Noah cruising
the Seven Seas in an ark
full of coupled creatures
tupping two by two
in the dark, the skipper, no
gambler, and unbefuddled
by oceans askew, saved
the world for Ham and Heaven.

High

For Sandra Ann Grocott

Sandy was my first romance,
a summer soireė of hand-
holding and curt kisses,
when we danced double
and strolled the boulevards,
shawling for shocked nods,
and I strutted about the streets
like a godling in rut: high
on hormones and eye-candy.

Thorns

Each summer morn,
across the street, I follow
the straw bonnet of the Widow
Bray floating above
her flawless flowers in a
bee-buffed breeze,
and she seems pleased with the
garden she grows to ease
the grip of her grief, knowing
full well that every
rose has thorns.

God's Good Humour

After a dust-up with his dam,
Noah set forth, unanchored,
onto a sea rumoured
to be shy of islands, in an ark
crammed with heathen beasts
and Ham, banking on God's
good humour to find him
a world, and save mankind.

Stuck

I never put much truck
in girls until one of them
harpooned my heart, and I loved
Maybelle from afar
like Romeo his Juliet, marooned
on a balcony, and I gazed at the
white-picket fence
upon which she preened
pristinely, and at the supple
swelling where I dreamt her new-
minted breasts slept,
and I longed to pledge my troth
like Lancelot his lady, but my tongue
tripped on itself, and stuck.

Tooth and Claw

Outside my window,
breathless in the breeze, a hawk
hangs, glides on eddies
of air and, with a looped
swoop, petrifies its prize
and widows its mate, with feathered
fury before lofting on wings
wedded to the wind, and I am
reminded of that old saw:
Nature: red in tooth
and claw.

Wintering

Bereaved of its leaves, this
maple in my fallen yard
stares bare-boned
into a sky, clotted with cloud
in the wilting light from a sun
bereft of its summer heft,
and in this time
of fallowed fields and the fringing
of frosts, we trust in the Earth's
rebirth, when bulbs bulge
with soon-to-be blooms
and robins throb with the nurturing
need and April rains
seize the sleeping seed
and waken it whole to the world,
but it is come Autumn now
and, ever a sinner, I must
winter over my soul.

Squeeze

The Reverend Bell assured us
God so loved the world
He gave us His only begotten
Son, but I had other
thoughts: girls with tender
breasts, and smiles that made
my loins loiter in their throbbing
sockets, and hockey games
where I, improbably, scored
the winning goal, awed
by the elixir of applause, and so
it was I did my best
to squeeze Jesus into my heathen
heart.

Arrival

At Autumn's arid arrival
the leaves of summer subside
in a slow mellowing before
the fire inside, and robins
dream the sunny South
in the gist of their genes, and geese
have a yen to seize the first
convenient breeze and ride it,
and asters outlast the lapsing
of light, and April's rose
comes undone,
and labouring bees evict
the drones and coddle the Queen,
and apples quicken in their trees,
threatening to fall, and school-
children ponder foolscap,
waiting for words to stipple
into stories about the season
when all things Earthen
malinger before silently
singing the advent of birth
and beginning.

Dixie

We hopped in your silver Volks
and jogged off to Big Town,
when you took a country bumpkin
and introduced him to the opera
with sopranos in ball gowns
and tenors in tux, and we promenaded
down Avenue Road
as if we might have been lovers
seducing the world: you
with your pointillist pumps
and me in my Sunday clogs,
picking straw from my teeth
and whistling Dixie.

Marooned

Mrs. Bradley, marooned
on her front stoop, lets loose
such a cry of anguish and unhope
that it's heard at the village verges,
and she can't tell rubber from rope
or hers from his, and wonders
where on Earth she is.

When Love Harrows

When love harrows the heart,
all thought of the self
is urged upon the other,
and there is no art
as ardent as the dance of desire,
that elfin fandango
when the soul surges aloft
and narrows on the nearest star

Mooch

My dog Moochie rhymed
with pooch, a water spaniel
with webbed feet and no
pool to paddle in,
who assailed passing autos
as if he could bark them to death,
who followed me to school
as if I were the Pied Piper,
where he mooched his lunch on the
front steps, and when
he fell mortally ill,
my father drove him to the
countryside and dropped him
there, alone and intestate,
and I wondered if he might
have met someone
who loved dogs more than
the cost of a vet.

Wings

Outside my window
the trees are de-leafing,
there is an autumnal hum
to the wind and all things
summer come undone,
and though I have no heart
for what Winter brings,
I remain steadfast
in my belief that Spring will glide
into bloom on welcoming wings.

Galleon

For Grace Leckie

I dithered by the wayside,
waiting for Grace to ride by
on her roan stallion, her prized
thighs gripping its gallop,
and when she deigned to wave,
my heart went striding apace,
and I felt like a chuffed buccaneer
counting gold on his galleon.

Fledgling

Mrs. Bray says
her prayers every night,
asking the All-Mighty
to let her fledgling flowers
bloom full-petalled
in glancing light, and then
she lays her head upon
a pillow and dreams perchance
of daisies and daffodils.

Marybelle

Marybelle Cooper, my best
friend's cousin, lingered
long enough at our picket
fence to be opulently
observed in her green tartan,
feathering her brand-new
breasts, and when she smiled
in my direction, my heart
did cartwheels and my nether
parts went cock-a-hoop.

The Day I Fell in Love

I was idling by the curb, awaiting
your imminent arrival, while a brief
breeze hummed autumnal
in the trees and a robin throbbed
with song and a morning dove
on the neighbouring lawn bided
her time, and I recall each
detail of that October morning
when the sun shone celibate
in a sky shorn of cloud,
and there you were, whirring
up in your silver Volks,
tangerine locks flung
free as you stepped out
like a queen bee brandishing
the buzz of her hive, your lemon
frock and upswept tresses
making a believer out of me,
and in that monumental moment
I knew what love was.

Fiefdom

This maple outside
my window, bleeds
crimson, whetted by the whims
of an Autumn wind, and in
the seed seething in its leafage
are intimations of Spring,
when, having defied the wince
of Winter, roots, bevelling
below, hunger for Summer
and the rinse of rain, and in the
circling of the seasons we are assured
the fiefdom of the Earth will endure.

Local

Whenever I think of the Point,
I imagine a place that drew me
full-blooded into the world,
where poems grew fantastical
on trees made lyrical
by light, where budding bards
could fletch and fly and be
anointed laureate of the local,
groomed for greatness, and where
home was its own season.

Beyond Blood and Bone

There are times when we make a fetish
of flesh, when a man gazes
at his girl and sees only
breast and buttock or a woman
eyes the muscled lust
of her lover, and beauty itself
is more than the honing of poems,
than Picasso's cubic runes,
or what Michelangelo
amazed into marble:
it breeds in the genes, and lets us
live beyond the boundaries
of blood and bone.

Spare Parts

O Nancy Mara, you broke
my heart before I knew
what true romance was,
and, like Abelard, I loved from afar,
as chaste as Eloise in her nunnery,
and I might have been the one
if only I had spoken my love,
but my tongue was tied when
your gliding glances stunned
my spare parts.

Rinsed

Every day the Widow Bray
prays for rain to rinse
her garden and set the buds
a-bloom, and ease the pain
of her bereavement, and her flowers,
unhurried, grow
abundant in God's eyes,
as if He weren't satisfied
with merely reproducing
Eden in this domestic
domain, and under His benevolent
skies and undulating breezes,
she hasn't had a worry,
then or since.

Neighbourhood

In this dream
Tom and I walk
the village verge to verge,
and I point to the window where
I first welcomed the world
in and where I lay abed
rheumatic for seven months,
dreaming of plots and doings
for novels yet to be,
and we stroll down to the docks
where my Dad and I poached
perch and watched the lakers
steam by, aimed at anywhere,
and we followed the shoreline
to Canatara and the Saharan
sweep of its beach, and Tom
smiles and nods, pleased
to know the place that seemed
to me as big as the Earth's
girth but small enough
to squeeze into an apprentice poem,
and we both thank the good
gods for bringing us here
to share the neighbourhood
I've always called home.

Truce

We dubbed her Juicy Joyce
before we knew a thing
about the gentle gender
or what aspect of her anatomy
we had in mind (and whether
it was tough or tender), but when
I passed her in the litter
of her yard, I did my best
to be kind and keep my eyes
averted from the bud between
her thighs, and when my mates
gave voice to their mocking moniker,
I demurred, and called for a truce.

A Walk in the Park

Walking is a way of saying
"Hello" to the world, to Gibbon's
in all its green glory,
where squirrels squander
up and down the trunks
of trees that still remember
a century of summers, and an owl
peers from a low limb,
and one of the 'regulars' nods
with his deerstalker cap,
and on the river, rippled
by a bright breeze, a heron
leans and sips, and a golden
carp jumps over itself
and a kingfisher darts
for his dinner, and I keep on
walking till I wear out
my welcome or the story ends.

Gusts

In Hendrie's derelict coop
we played the game of "chicken"
with our private parts, and Jo
bared her brand-new
breasts for our amusement,
then dropped her pants
to expose the doozy, dozing
where her belly began,
and a cheer went up from the boys
between gusts of lust,
and nobody cared that we were
all shrewdly nude
and girls were born to break
our hearts.

Groomed

The Widow Bray's blooms
lusted after light and its
pertinent probing, and obeyed
every tingle of her touch,
and when she bid them propagate,
such was her passion for
horticulture and its pains-
taking demand, she was soon
as ease with her bereavement
and groomed, at last, for gaiety.

Aglow:
Waterloo County October 1961

You take me walking on the Doon
Pinnacle on a June evening
embroidered with stars and a moon
that lavishes our path with lunar
light, and you fold my hand
in yours as if we might
have been lovers, and I loiter,
list to leeward, afraid
to breathe lest you dissolve
shapeless into shadow, hold
this moment intact,
until your face gets wreathed
aglow, and our eyes greet,
and you smile as wide as
any horizon.

Soothed

Grandfather's yard was all
my world when I was young
enough to know better:
with a lawn as looming as a lake
and two tall trees
where sunlight lived
in the breeze-licked leaves
and lilacs hung dozing
in droops and honey-bees
noshed on nectar where lilies
bloomed in petalled puffs
and snowdrops teemed
hectic in the hedges that hugged
my world home, and when
I tired of innocence, I lay me
down and soothed myself
with bardic dreams.

Strolling Canatara

I take you strolling
on Canatara, where sea-
grasses weep in the on-
shore breeze that soothes
the dunes in their swivelled fluting
and sweetens the sand squeezing
our feet, and overhead
the afternoon sun
breathes lambent light
and herring gulls careen,
and out on the Lake, rollers
consume themselves
and the furred horizon hazes,
and we arrive where the beach
demurs, and I take your hand
as if days like this
were enough to keep you alive.

At Home

Poetry is in the gist of our genes,
a distillation of what
we cannot know and find
the words to say, a means
of arrogating Beauty to our prudent
use, of pinning whatever
moment we feel in the prism
of a poem, in the serendipity
of its simile, in the torque of its metaphor,
and in these hopeful tropes
we go where the heart is most
at home.

Bid

The Widow Bray bid
"Good monring" to her flowers
and moved among her daffodils
and daisies like Gaia garnishing
her humble Greek garden,
and won the praise of half
the town for her Green Thumb
and countless hours lived
amid things that grew
anew whenever touched
by her taut, untarnished hand

On the Wane

The Widow Bray tends
her groomed garden, grieving
at every petal gone
a-droop, and when the summer's
roses are on the wane
and autumn's leaves incline,
she dreams of daffodils
and May bouquets in her
living room, and an end
to her bereavement pain.

Bellow

In Sunday School we sang
of Jesus bidding us shine
and God's spared sparrow
and the little light we let
live in our small corner
and thine, and we rang the rafters
raw, our voices swollen
with the Holy Ghost
and a hatful of Hallelujahs,
and I wanted to come to attention,
salute and bellow "Rule Britannia"!

Ballet

For Tom in loving memory and for Zak Gordon

Rugby is a game of ballet
and body blows, of tug-
hugging scrums and the
occasional kick at a ball
that floats like a wounded duck,
of turf-lurch and mud-
wallow and quickening sprints,
and you grapple with the best
of them, knowing I'm following
every torque and tackle,
marooned on the sideline
like a doting uncle, and negotiating
with the gods of Luck, my heart
in my throat.

Our Team

In Sunday School we were told
that Our Saviour suffered us
to come unto Him, that the Lord's
house had many mansions,
and when the organ wheezed out
The Doxology, our voices went soaring
to the beams above, for we were
certain we were on the Jesus
team.

Bridal

The Widow Bray's feelings
for her blooms bordered on the
libidinous, for she doted on her
daffodils like a hovering lover,
stroked her roses till they ripened,
turned the April earth
over with an amorous hand
and spent her days and hours
ordering this petal
or kissing that one, as bright
as a bride in her flowered
bower.

Into the April Morning

I step out into the April
morning like Adam introducing
himself to Eden, the crocuses
just nudging their pouting
snouts into the everywhere
ambience of the air, and under
a hedge, ferns unfurl
like phallic fans and purple
iris flog their favours
and lilac buds bulge
towards bloom and daffodils,
long enbulbed, break
their maiden in the fertile forge
of the sun. and I feel a poem
poke up pulsing inside,
and my words, April-aged,
find at last a voice,
palpitating on the page.

Green World

Spring was in its infancy:
crocuses poked their petalled
snouts into the erogenous air
and tulip bulbs broke
erotic at the seams and nippled
shoots enthused in an incendiary
sun and lactating buds
bruised the bantering breeze –
and I walked out into this
green world like Adam
carrying the genes of Eden,
like Cain proving fratricidal,
like Moses reading the desert
runes, like Homer dreaming
Odysseys, my head bursting
with April words, my bardic
body engroined by poems.

Date

Shirley doing the fan-
dance on Grandfather's lawn,
showing a curve of calf
and an intimate inch of thigh,
twirling her mother's boa
and shaking her garden gate,
as if she were old enough
to be billing and cooing
and we had nerve enough
to ask her for a date.

Bridal

The Widow Bray's feelings
for her blooms bordered on the
libidinous, for she doted on her
daffodils like a hovering lover,
stroked her roses till they ripened,
turned the April earth
over with an amorous hand
and spent her days and hours
ordering this petal
or kissing that one, as bright
as a bride in her flowered
bower.

A Love Poem

On Honeymoon Bay we pitch
our tent and watch it rise
like a birthday balloon,
and we listen to wavelets purring
along the shoreline,
and marvel at the dew-gilded
grass and shadows breeding
in the dark, and I am stunned
by the star-shine in your eyes,
mirroring the firmament above,
and we are sung to sleep
by the cove's even breathing
and, cocooned, we embrace
our bodies, and I feel no need
to say I love you.

Fifteen for Anne

For Anne in loving memory

Furious Felicity

I wake in your arms once
again, unforsaken,
and even though I know
I'm dreaming, I hug you
like the last Adam in Eden
offering Eve a paradisal
pass to the celibate sun,
and I want to tell you
there are gods that keep us
from harm's way, from being
a delegate to Death, and that love
with its furious felicity redeems
us all, but that would be
a luxurious lie, for such
deities let me love
and you, die.

Vistas

When you whispered "I love you
too," the syllables sang
in my soul, and O how long,
locked in my loneliness and gauche
among girls, I yearned to hear
those words, and lose myself
in emotion's arable ocean
like a ripening rose succumbed
with sun or a dolphin seized
in the sea's surround or blue-
birds marooned in the gist
of a breeze, and I wanted to sing you
sonnets to make the Bard
blush and brandish your beauty
in ballads that rhymed as precise
as prisms and promise you vistas
of gibbous moons and serene
dreams.

Vintage

Love was ever our addiction,
and we indulged it as licit
as any two lovers
in the honey months or Abelard
in his wistful missives to Eloise
untupped in her tower or Lancelot
eyeing the prim and gainly
Guin or Romeo jousting
for Juliet, and our romance bulged
blissful, out-blued
the blues for fifty-seven
years, and we let it age
like oak-soaked vintage
until Death asked you to dance
and you were too polite
to refuse.

Numinous

I wake into this room
emptied of you, and gaze
at the night-sky illumed
by a connubial moon, and I
recall another evening
when we strolled Dune Pinnacle
under a firmament stirred
by stars, and our love was presumed
anew in that numinous hour,
was more than illusion and never
in doubt, even when the
bloom bled out.

Moonstruck

You watered and fed me
for fifty-seven years
and I'd like to thank the good
gods for bringing you willing
into my world, where our shared love
lingered, even when the bloom
buckled, and you, O daughter
of Demeter and all things
earthen, gave birth to the dappled
days of my happiness, had the rare gift
of giving, led me easing
into my age, and now, too soon
gone, have left me like a loon
without a lake, but still,
against the odds, moonstruck.

Longitudes

You were always camera-shy,
as if that elemental eye
could never capture
the essence that soared inside,
or perhaps you were merely modest,
letting others gather
in the glow of the limelight,
but photo-ed or not, you were the
star of my firmament, the moon
of my misbegotten nights
and the joy of our conjugal communion,
but now you reside somewhere
in those vast longitudes
above the fray, where I hope
you sing your soul free,
and abide.

Free

Love is what we feel
but cannot touch, the ache
that makes us tender,
and I wanted so much
to hold you whole, embrace
every breath of your being
and heal whatever hurt,
letting your body be,
and above all and against
the odds, have your soul
sing free.

Harmony

When you drove your silver
Volks to the curb on that
tic-toc October
morn, my heart held
its breath, and I was impressed
by the feminine lemon of your dress
and the upswept tresses
that would have shamed a carrot,
and I chose you before you
chose me, and I bless the day
we met halfway in helpless
harmony.

Buzz

with a nod to Emily Dickinson

The night you died, I thought
I heard a bee buzz
outside your doomed room
 like Emily's unmuzzled
fly, and when my plot
plays out, I hope to go
before my mind does.

Id

I wake and imagine your body
once again nestled
next to mine, and you bid me
batten on your breasts, for whenever
our souls sagged or lost
their legs, ours was a carnal
acquaintance, when we traded
egos for an id.

Unexempt

I wake from a troubled sleep.
having dreamt you are still
alive, your body a brief
breath away, its warmth
leaving a lustre on mine,
my heartbreak suddenly
doubled, for I am alone
in a room emptied of you,
unexempt from bereavement's
bite, and while it may be
true we are groomed for grief,
love is deeper than dying.

Ardour

You left me without a nod
or the blessing of a goodbye,
and I wanted the last words
to earnest your ears to be
"I love you still," and to take you
by the hand and walk you
willing and unalone
into the deepening dark,
and I must confess I felt
the tug of our love too strong
for us ever to be parted,
and I'd like to thank the good
gods for bringing you
singing into my soul,
and I want to keep you clinging
there as we once were,
hug you with the ardour
of my heart, and then set you
free and easing into
your long sleep.

Compromise

You loved me to the hilt
with the lilting bent of your being,
and when the need arose,
you cradled my lust, knowing
we belong best to our bodies,
and when the world built up
too much in our eyes,
I laid my head upon
your breast just so,
and we compromised.

Joust

Once again you bedevil
my dream and we are abed,
your body bevelling mine,
your warmth a wooled welcome
as we reenact our wedding
night like lovers learning
the tacticity of touch
and the conjugal joys of our Faustian
jousting, and I want so much
to redream the long, liberating
years of our love, untouched
by the tyrannies of Time, redeemed
by two souls singing
their solos— in rhyme.

Legacies

You come to me in the
dark heart of the night,
when I am dreading the dream
in which you wave goodbye
as if you were going somewhere
else than the domain
of the dead and its aborted bliss,
and we would meet again
in moonlight like lovers
in the honey month, and plumb
the legacies of love and make
each other immortal.

Fifty for Tom

In loving memory

A Summer Day

In this recurring dream
you and I walk out
into a June morning,
soothed by sunshine
licking the lavender loveliness
of lilacs, and we agree
that summer is our season,
when everything greens
and plumps, when hatchlings feel
the wind widen under
their wings, and meadowlarks
sing as if song itself
sanctified their belonging,
and squads of starlings blur
the far horizon, and in the grass
between the trees an adder
seethes from side to side,
and you remark that Beauty
is not beholden to the eye
but to the soul that hearkens,
and I do not wish the dream
to darken and find that you
have died.

Livid

I remember you most in the mornings,
when the sun, new-born,
pours its warmth over
my wakened world like honey
from a bee-teased comb,
bedewing field and flower
and sending my blood into bloom
with thoughts of you, home
and the poems I'll compose
aright about the love
we shared like a rich rose,
livid with light, and I love you
again come evening,
when the moon, marooned in the island
of the sky, glows with mellowed
beam, and I hear you singing
in my dreams.

Faith

I've often wondered where souls
go when they abandon the body,
and whether some semblance
of you, some ember of your having been,
is floating this side
of the Heaven I'v tried to believe in
since my Sunday-School certainties
(and the hymns of hope we learned
by rote) bid me dream
of resting among the angels
when I died, and saying hello
to the Prince of Paradise,
but my faith, never more
than knee-deep, has faltered
and I must be content with having
your soul sing in my sleep

This Day

Tom and I walking
the woods above Cyprus,
hugged by cedar and fir
and the silt of centuries, where
orchards of orchids blow
blue and gold in the teasing
breeze, and on the matted
path we trod, a rattler
unwraps and glides into the
grass and jays jostle
like bossy gossips and a
titmouse tilts on a twig
and in the undergrowth a badger
blunders and a weasel stints
its victim, and down in the swamp
bullfrogs entertain like big-
bellied bassos, and we feel
as we go the tug of love,
and thank the glee-gods,
wherever they be, for granting us
such a land.

Mellow

Outside my window,
the season comes autumnal:
maple trees: leafless
and agape, their bruised roots
reaching deep for a last
dram, and burrowed beasts
dream of slow sleep
on the brink of November days
and umbered skies, and I too
find my mood un-
summered, thinking of you
marooned where no light
lives and of the time
when you could radiate a room,
when your smile beckoned
and beguiled, when your wit lit up
my life, and never again
will you see a solstice swivel
the Earth or a harvest moon
mellow.

Hazard

When we hazard love
with the livid wick of our soul,
we weigh the possibility of loss
against the heft of affection,
the sweet ache of romance
or the cost of uncaring,
and so it was, you arrived
at our bailiwick like an emissary
from the green serenes of Eden,
etched innocent and graced
with a giving heart, and we
were forever limned by love
and the risks we dared to take.

Agape

Outside my window
this maple seethes
leaves, as crimson as a
cardinal's cape, as golden
as Bligh's doubloons limned
in light, and I feel the ache
of Autumn agape in my bones,
for you are gone lonely
into your grave, where no love
thrives, will never see
the pied glory of a season's
surrender, nor know that your loss
has left me unalive..

Going

When I first saw you
in that incubator
taking baby breaths,
your wee fingers still
wizened from the womb, glancing
off any horizon,
I didn't think we'd see you
growing golden into your bones,
but we did, and you grew anew
each loving day
you gave us, and when Death
drew you into its darkness,
we mourned your lonely going,
knowing you would never be old.

Majestic

When you talked tenderly
of my poems and stories, I was moved
by the majesty of your mind and the tenor
of your tact when a plot meandered
or a rhyme failed to chime,
and you felt the loneliness of the love
I brought to the work of a life-
time, where I sang solo
to a disembodied audience,
but found a home in your rightful
reading, and I want to thank
the Muse-endued gods
who gave me the gift of your patient
giving, I now brandish
as a badge of our brief belonging.

Brevity

Once again we are walking
the woods above Cyprus,
admiring the bark of a birch,
ripened white in the sun's
stark slant, and wild
orchids too shy
to parade their wind-puffed
petals in the occasional lancing
of light overhead, and we laugh
at the disputatious jays
palavering about perches and the
kneading of seeds, and watch
in awe as a Massasauga
ripples across our path
and see-saw its way
to the swamp, where bull-frogs
snog in the heat-haze,
and we marvel at the wonder of these
halcyon days and ponder
the ever-lapsing of love
and life's unbenevolent
brevity.

Seasons

The soul too has its seasons:
erupting in April like bulb-
burst and rupturing root,
sunning itself serene
in the lustre of May-limned
light, and cruising nude
through the petall'd hues of June.
And then settling into Summer,
where it ripens like a seed-seething
pomegranate, hums among
bee-numbed blooms,
and dapples appling orchards,
unbitten by blight.
And then it comes autumnal
when trees bleed leaves
as pied as a painter's palette
and snowbirds feel
an inkling in their wings and squirrels
forage for the nip of nuts
and all things slide
towards the silos of sleep.
And then, having worn out
its welcome, it winces into
wintering weather, where my soul
now sits like a frozen rose,
to be untethered whenever
I recall the miracle of a May
morning or remember your saying
we are all the sum of our gaieties
and griefs, and that love is the best
reason for being born.

Odes

When the world goes fallow
and trees sleep in the arms
of a summering breeze and robins
swallow the song in their throats
and crickets freeze in the grip
of grass and silence grows
unechoed, deepening
into itself, I can hear
your soul singing from that
bleak abode you now
inhabit. and I long to tell you
across the great divide
how much I miss your elfin
grin, the way you smiled
with your eyes and the vim
in your voice when appraising a poem,
and now that you have died
I am resigned to soliciting silence
and penning odes to those I have lost.

Beryl

We love at our peril: when we
share our most secret
self with another, caring
not that we tingle on a trapeze
without a net, that the heart
might get hurt in love's
silken seizures, but we are all
born duly nude
before we're armoured against
the world's unsoothing
intrusion or the aftereffects
of affection denied, but I loved you
from the moment I saw your elfin
grin and the smile you made
with the blue beryl of your eyes,
and I hope wherever you are
love still abides.

Jewelled

When I was almost young
and lilacs hung on the hedges
like jewelled jasmine, and I wandered
the acre'd lake of Grandfather's
lawn (where dandelions dawdled
in the morning-born light)
like a sailor seeking the sea's
secret, and I wanted to bring you
here where I was etched in innocence,
and show you the place where my poems
first geysered seamless into being,
when words sprung anew
in my universe in petall'd
pandemonium, and you
would nod, recognizing the root
of all rhyming, and I would thank
the good gods for letting me
love you, and promise to forgo
a hundred dawns to have you
whole and with me once again.

In the Bone

In this dream, you and I
are perambulating the pristine
sands of Canatara and its soothing
dunes, and walking the sun-
strummed streets where I first
found reasons for my feet,
and I want to show off
the village that bore me up
like a bard's breath in the throes
of procreation, and I point out
the green desmene of Grandfather's
lawn and the milkweed
meadow where butterflies buffed
themselves buoyant on the breeze
and garter snakes combed
creases in the marsh grasses
and the Bridge hovered over
the town like a lunatic lover,
and out of this wizard's womb
I honed a universe of verse,
bone-deep and thudding
in the blood.

Throttled

And love too is an addiction,
you never gave up on it,
and fought against the angst
of that alcohol-itch,
and O how I wish you'd found
someone constant enough
to pour your love upon
and share your evening days,
for in the end it turned
inward, brewing in the blood
like a throttled tongue, and
with no voice to give it
direction, it fed upon
itself like a self-deriding
demon, and died.

Prime

You were just in the summer
of your living, that time
of year when all things
Earthen fatten in the field
or bulge voluptuous on the vine,
when hatchlings a month from birth
feel the wind widen
under their wings and poppies
preen in the ripening sun
and the breeze hums
with bee-buzz and lark-
lyric, and we thought, like a
dozing rose lusting
after light, you would glide
into the bloom of your manhood,
but something in the bud
must have soured, crippling
the flower, and leaving it to perish
in its prime.

Stung

When you were young and I was
yet to be wise, and roses
hung unbudding
on our backyard arbour,
we shared a single story,
breeding dreams of Spring
and its harbouring of hope,
at ease with our genes and pleased
to let our mutual garden
grow eloped by love,
but you lived only half
your allotted Summers, benumbed
by addiction and leaving me
among whatever memories
you etched upon my breath –
stung by your derelict demise.

Autumns

This maple in my yard
bleeds crimson just
before its leaves unlatch,
and I am reminded that all
things fall, that we live
at the whim of the winds that blow
our seasons to and fro,
and even the prized tree
carries the seeds of its own
demise and bends its breezes
to other ends, and Winter
is where we go when the soul
sours, but you were merely
a hatchling, gliding into the
summer of your life with no
reason to succumb and should
have lived to see a hundred
leaf-tossed autumns.

Brave

Your final months were troubled
as you struggled with the angst
of addiction, but you were brave
beyond your years and never
gave up on loving, the twinkle
in your eye never dimmed,
and your smile could still rescue
a room, and you remained
the hub of my happiness, and now
that you are gone into that grim
abode where no love resides,
we, the living, must let you
go, consigning you
to memories that enrich, and abide.

Abode

I'd like to glide into
that sloe abode, that bone-
yard of belonging, that doomed
dark where no love
abides and souls are cleaved
by grief, that drew you witting
into it, and bring you un-
departed, back to me,
but death is more daunting
than our desires, and you
have left me marooned in a
world I never made, alone
with a ransacked heart.

All Things

Like all things that love
the light, your soul sang
its own song, fuelled
by its own fire, and you let it
live where desire abides,
and in the unbelonging
of the night, let it brighten
as it died.

Teem

For Tn this dream, I take you
walking in the milkweed
meadow abutting grand-
father's yard, where hoppers
catapult in the wisping
grasses, an adder un-
braids in the sizzle of the sun,
Monarchs tip-toe
on puckered pods with their silken
insides, larks lullaby
the breeze with a summer song,
dragonflies dart diaphanous,
and a kildeer struts his belonging,
and out on the marsh, cattails
moult on stiffened stalks,
and we are content to let
the day drift and our hearts teem

Glisten

I listen to Belafonte
singing "Danny Boy"
and in that singular soaring
I feel the joy of your presence
once more, your soul
lucent in that elegiacal
lilt, and I marvel at the
power of song to focus
our feelings and make our tears
glisten.

Buoyant

None of us can dodge Death
through we bob and weave
to keep the blood buoyant,
and you bravely fought the angst
of your addiction down to the final
twitch, and never gave up
loving, kept it lodged
in the hub of your heart, though
we all go solo
into the last goodbye,
I hope on the way you were sung
home by the cheers of cherubim
and a choir of hovering angels,
leaving me to mourn:
my grief, a lonely lover.

Baptism

I wish that you had lived
one more day
so that I could've taken you
fishing for a final time
on Cameron's crystalline lake,
where the bass are biting like
barracuda on a binge,
and the afternoon sun
gilds us with luminous light,
and in a far cove, a blue
heron tilts on a solitary
stilt, yellow-billed
mallards manoeuvre smoothly
and loons cruise, and on
this anondyne day
we are blessed baptismal, tinged
with love's wistful wizardry,
while overhead herring
gulls are crying: "Let there
be no more dying."

Dream

Cameron was groomed out of granite
forty thousand years
ago, when Cro-Magnon
and his simian cousins roamed
the combes and valleys of the Earth
and side-stepped the great
glacial glide, giving
birth as it vanished, and these
artesian waters were waiting
just for us on a sun-
thrummed June afternoon,
as if the geological gist
of history held no meaning
for us, for we were here
like those ancient anglers,
patrolling for Pisces on a lake
that seemed like a dream of itself.

Muppetry

O how we loved the Muppets!
chesterfield chums, we sat
in front of the TV
enthralled by such madcap
puppetry, such tangled
tomfoolery, and you
were appalled when the Critics
belittled Fosse Bear or booed
the bedroom drama
of Bert and Ernie, and delighted
when Miss Piggy jiggled
across the screen for her star
turn, and of course we adored
Kermit the Frog with a voice
like a crushed walnut, hogging
the limelight, and we rode
the same train of laughter
and wry raillery, and I thought
then I would not live long
enough to see you die.

Hallowed

Tom and I angling
for rainbow on Cameron
like St. Peter trolling
for souls on Galilee
or Izaak's daughter trawling
for Dad, the silence around us
cathedral deep, the afternoon
stroked by a celibate sun,
and we feel blessed to be here,
afloat on the blue beauty
of our lake and on these
hallowed billows, where
any moment I expect to see
Jesus walking on water.

One Wish

If I had one wish
left after a lifetime
of calling on the good will
of the granting gods, it would be
to go fishing once
more with you on Cameron
on a summer's afternoon,
celibate with sunlight,
trolling for jut-jawed
bass, frantic on the hook
in the dappled dells below,
and suffering the hours to drift by,
like Adam contemplating
a meandered brook in Eden
(before the apple interrupted),
and we were at ease with our interim
innocence and a bond buttressed
bright by love.

Above Cyprus

Above Cyprus we are welcomed
into woods where wild orchids
flutter like shy surprises
and a Massasauga seesaws
through the undergrowth
towards the swamp where bullfrogs
bulge and, in a beaver meadow,
butterflies tease the breeze
on wobbling wings and blue
jays jostle for the perfect
perch, and we are hugged
happily by spruce and cedar
and birch with their alabaster
bark a-gleam in sunlight
falling through the trees
like the drift of a dream, and we
meander as if the gift
of this day would last
as long as we hearken to its
heartbeat, and love.

Possibility

Cameron Lake, July 1995

Our afternoon is ambered by a
hazy sun, the daylight
moon a silver sliver
nearby, we are sitting in Uncle's
boat, fishing lines
a-droop, ringed by a shrug
of cedars, the silence between us
wordless, as easy as breathing,
soon a brightening breeze
stirs wavelets that nosh
on our gunwales, overhead
in a pristine sky herring
gulls gossip, among
the trees jays fraternize,
and in fisherman's cove,
a loon manoeuvres, and we think
there exists both love
and the possibility of perfection

Such Days

Once again we find
ourselves walking the woods
above Cyprus, where squirrels
stir the undergrowth,
blue jays bicker,
a hawk hangs and a white-
tail startles the dark
where the sun balks, and our talk
is all of poems and their passionate
propensities and of fiction
that scratches the itch of our humanity,
and my thoughts drift towards
mortality and the brevity of our being,
how little time there is
to share such unmatchable
days as these, when walking is
a way of saying, "I love you."

Someone Else

From the moment I mouthed your name,
an hour after your de-wombing,
that singular syllable
sang on my tongue like a divo
singing solo, and whenever
I touched a portion of the room
you reserved for all things loving,
you grew anew in my eyes,
but now that you are gone
into that bleak abode
where no light lives,
I have such a need
for long goodbyes
and someone else to blame.

Never Enough

I was there when you were just
unwombed and taking
incubator breaths,
and I smiled at the melodious
lallings from your crib one
room away, and I watched
your maiden steps and the grin
you gave me when teetered
upright, and I marvelled at the first
words you uttered, like petite
poems from a bard's tongue
upon my avid ear,
and I cheered on, with a stuttering
heart, your ad-libbing rugby
moves and Gretzkian gestures,
and I loved you alive
for all the years of our living,
in the good times and the rough,
but Death has dominion and love
is never enough.

Meadow

In this dream we are walking
the milkweed meadow
abutting Grandfather's lawn,
and our talk is of butterflies
munching lactating leaves
and thick-lipped pods,
and mourning doves fluttering
free of gravity's grip,
and an oriole's artful aria
wisping on eddies of air,
and, tickling the grass with the jut
of his tongue, an adder fresh
from Eden, and as we ease
into evening, you remark that we
are all redeemed by acts
of love, and I'd trade a hundred
dawns to have you here
again in the harbour of my heart.

Cherished

You cherished Cameron the moment
your eyes alighted on its loveliness,
and you paddled in its shallows like a
slim-finned dolphin,
and we lazed away amber
afternoons angling
for behemoth bass with a bite
like a barracuda, cruising
the blue glades below
(the sun above like a detonated
Doubloon), and we felt like Adams
idling in Eden, and those
days seemed to be
forever, as if we could outwit
the world, as if our poems
were raids on the redoubts
of Reason, as if love were
not the hub of our happiness,
as if I would not live
seasons enough to see
you perish.

Milestone

Once again I dream you
alive, and we are in
that room we set aside
for poetry palaver and teasing
the meaning out of books
we might have overlooked,
and the talk this day
is of the Dickensian characters
quickening my fiction and whether
I've perused Faulkner or the Gothics,
and when you read aloud
my poem "Galilee," our voices
merge and, for a breathless second,
we are one another, purged
of envy and ego, and I wanted you
then to ripen into your age,
see your sons salute
the next century and be
a milestone for my memory,
where Death is just another
season.

Pedigrees

I always thought that I
would go before you
because age has its exigencies,
that I would drift into the darkness
that swallows us all, knowing
you would grow old with grace
and gravity, would sow your genes
into the next century, and live
to tell the world of a man
humbled by multitudinous
words, who spun his poems
and stories out of a love
for the home ground and a passion
for roots and pedigrees, and now
that you are gone where no
grass gleams, my heart
is hollowed out, and my words,
benumbed, wither on the page.

Insurrection

I remember the afternoons
we spent playing in that rugg'd
room upstairs, pretending
we were afloat on a motionless
ocean and dabbling in our Duplo,
and I felt the tug of affection
in every grin you gave me,
as if we were groomed for this,
and I thought we would never be
apart, that you would not leave me
grieving, knowing that love
is an insurrection of the heart.

Good Night

You were only ten
when you fell in love with Cameron's
blue beauty, its cedar-
hugged shores and breeze-
brushed billows, and cradled
a fishing rod for the first
time, and we set out
each mist-drifted
morning for the dappled
dells where bass thrashed
and pickerel pounced on their prey,
and we sat side by side
savouring the silence that dwarfed
the distance between us,
and when the big one
struck with a tug like a terrapin
and lifted upright out of
its element like a sun-flung
rainbow, you reeled it in
like a pro in his prime, blessed
the god of all anglers, and gave me
a grin that has lasted a lifetime,
and I hope now that you did not
go lonely into Dylan's
Good Night.

When God's Stalked

Once again we find ourselves
among fir, spruce
and shawling cedar in the woods
above Cyprus, with sunlight
sifting through the screen of trees
and dappling our matted path,
and a brightening breeze plucks
at the petals of wild orchids,
shy in the sheltering shade,
and blue jays bicker
like unabridged barristers,
and nearby we catch a buzzing
of bees and their honeyed cousins,
and down at the grass-fringed
swamp, frog-song and the
clicking of crickets, and we watch
a brindled Massasauga
bend into the underbrush,
and we feel the amaze of this
place, where gods once
stalked and brontosaurus
walked upright into the
morning of the world, and in
your eyes I see reflected
the wonder of my own, and know
that none of use, prized
or outcast, is ever alone.

Back-Lit

For Tom in living memory

I see you still, seated
across the room from me
with a smile that would beguile
a misanthrope, eyes
back-lit with love
and a heart groomed for giving,
and I wanted to bend you into
the brunt of my embrace, for even
then I knew that losing you
would leave me without the hope
of happiness or the gentling of joy,
that my life would be forever
aborted, waiting for news
from the dead that you've been made
immortal.

Hug

Mara's lamp glows
with lassoed light from the moon
and its tidal tug, and we play
our hide-and-go-seek
on the shoulders of shadows and under
the gemmed embossing of stars,
the sexes pressed together
as if gender were something
too ample to be
denied, when the flesh fletches
and bodies, begging to be
bruised, hug the dark.

Homage

I was bred on Bible stories:
Adam and Eve gallivanting
in the Garden like nudes in a brooder,
red-lipped Delilah
snipping her lover's locks
and letting him die, eye-
blind in Gaza, David:
grounding Goliath with an
impertinent pebble, Shadrack
and the lads fanning themselves
with flame, Joshua: jumbling
Jericho with just the vim
of his voice, and Jesus pinned
on His cross like a freeze-dried
moth: these were the prudent
parables I gripped the grammar of
and hammered home in a score
of poems and more: with homage
due and a legacy of love.

Astride

Grace Leckie: astride
her roan stallion, the pummel
pulsing in the vise of her thighs,
and gripping the gallop, she passed
me by with a smile impishly
innocent, and I was numb
from the neck down, my fancy
fuelled by duelling thoughts:
a damsel with a dulcimer and co-
habiting horses in bestial
embrace.

Cousins

Grace Leckie sat
two rows over,
but close enough that I couldn't
take my eyes off
the swell in her sweater where
her breasts nested or off
the tartan skirt throttling
her thighs, and I thought of a
dozen ways I would introduce
myself to those puffed
lips and offer to be more
than kissing cousins, and we
would embrace like lovers too
foolish to be wise, at which
prudent point the daydream
died.

Fall

In Sunday School, I gave
my all for gentle Jesus
and the hope of Heaven, and sang
of God seeing the sparrow
fall, but at the time
I found it odd that He didn't
reach down with His catcher's
mitt, and save it.

Capture

Across two rows
and an aisle, I peered at Grace
in her best cashmere, under
which slept a brace
of breasts in raptured repose,
and when she beamed a smile
in my direction, more than my heart
was captured, and what I dreamed
that night, between tosses
and turns, would steam the hide
off a heifer and bring delight
to Mephistopheles.

O Beautiful Boy

For Tom in loving memory

O my beautiful boy!
you left me to go alone
into the undawning of my days
without the joy you engendered,
and never again will I hear
that voice across the room
we grew intimate in,
you: appraising my poems and stories
with tender tact and a critical
glint in your wise eye,
chuckling at the frantic antics
of my benighted family and fraught
forebears, and sharing the merest
sliver of your soul – and I am
doomed to an avalanche of emptiness
until your face floats
free of your dark demise
and mirrors mine, and I rejoice,
O beautiful boy!

About the Author

Don Gutteridge was born in Sarnia and raised in the nearby village of Point Edward. He taught High School English for seven years, later becoming a Professor in the Faculty of Education at Western University, where he is now Professor Emeritus. He has published seventy-one books: poetry, fiction and scholarly works in literary criticism and pedagogical theory and practice. He has published twenty-two novels, including the twelve-volume Marc Edwards mystery series, and thirty-eight books of poetry, one of which, Coppermine, was short-listed for the 1973 Governor-General's Award. In 1970 he won the UWO President's Medal for the best periodical poem of that year, "Death at Quebec." Don lives in London, Ontario.

To listen to interviews with the author, go to:
http://thereandthen.podbean.com.